Celtic
Prayers
of yesterday
and today

LION
Giftlines

Contents

Vision and Service

In Difficult Times

Angels All Around

Day and Night

In God's Presence

A Good Death

Blessings

God in Trinity

In name of Father,
In name of Son,
In name of Spirit,
Three in One.

I bind unto myself this day,
The strong name of the Trinity,
By invocation of the same,
The three in one and one in
three.

ST PATRICK

The Three Who are over me,
The Three Who are below me,
The Three Who are above me here,
The Three Who are above me yonder,
The Three Who are in the earth,
The Three Who are in the air,
The Three Who are in the heaven,
The Three Who are in the great
pouring sea.

CARMINA GADELICA

Father, cherish me,
Son cherish me,
Spirit cherish me,
Three all-kindly.

Three aid my hope,
Three aid my love,
Three aid mine eye,
And my knee from stumbling,
My knee from stumbling.

God our Father and Mother

O Being of life!
O Being of peace!
O Being of time,
and time without cease!
O Being, infinite, eternity!
O Being, infinite, eternity!

PRAYER FROM THE ISLAND OF BENBECULA

I believe, O God of all gods,
That Thou art the eternal Father
of life:
I believe, O God of all gods,
That Thou art the Eternal Father
of love.

There is a mother's heart
in the heart of God.

May the everlasting
Father himself
take you in his own
generous clasp,
in his own generous arm.

My Druid is Christ

Son of the clouds
Son of the stars
Son of the elements
Son of the heavens
Son of the Moon
Son of the Sun.

O king of kings!
O sheltering wings,
O guardian tree!
All, all of me,
Thou Virgin's nurseling,
rests in thee.

I adore not
the voice of birds,
Nor sneezing,
nor lots in this world,
Nor a boy, nor lots,
nor women:
My Druid is Christ,
the son of God,
Christ, Son of Mary,
the Great Abbot,
the Father, the Son,
and the Holy Ghost.

At the first cry of the first bird
They began to crucify Thee.
O cheek like a swan,
It were not right ever
to cease lamenting –
It was like the parting of day
from night.

My dearest Lord,
be thou a bright flame
before me,
be thou a guiding star
above me,
be thou a smooth path
beneath me,
be thou a kindly shepherd
behind me,
today and for evermore.

ST COLUMBA

There is no life in the sea,
There is no creature in the river,
There is naught in the firmament,
But proclaims His goodness.
Jesu! Jesu! Jesu!
Jesu who ought to be praised.

❧

There is no bird on the wing,
There is no star in the sky,
There is nothing
beneath the sun,
but proclaims his goodness.
Jesu! Jesu! Jesu!
Jesu who ought to be praised.

Holy Spirit, Wild Goose

Great Spirit,
Wild Goose of the Almighty
Be my eye in the dark places;
Be my flight in the trapped places;
Be my host in the wild places;
Be my brood in the barren places;
Be my formation in the lost places.

RAY SIMPSON,
COMMUNITY OF AIDAN & HILDA

Spirit of integrity,
you drive us into the desert
to search out our truth.
Give us clarity to know what is right,
and courage to reject what is
strategic;
that we may abandon the false
innocence
of failing to choose at all,
but may follow the purposes
of Jesus Christ.
Amen.

JANET MORLEY

O God, life-giving Spirit,
Spirit of healing and comfort,
of integrity and truth,
we believe and trust in you.
Warm-winged Spirit, brooding
over creation,
rushing wind and Pentecostal fire,
we commit ourselves to
work with you
and renew our world.

JANET MORLEY

God of Creation

I believe, O Lord and
God of the peoples,
That Thou art the creator
of the high heavens,
That Thou art the creator
of the skies above,
That Thou art the creator
of the oceans below.

℘

I believe, O Lord and
God of the peoples,
That Thou art He who created
my soul and set its warp.
Who created my body
from dust and from ashes,
Who gave to my body breath
and to my soul its possession.

He is the God of
heaven and earth,
of sea and rivers,
of sun and moon and stars,
of the lofty mountains
and the lowly valley,
The God above heaven
and under heaven.

Family and Home

Bless to me, O God,
the moon that is above me.
Bless to me, O God,
the earth that is beneath me.
Bless to me, O God,
my wife and my children.
And bless, O God,
myself who have
the care of them.

O God, bless my homestead,
Bless thou all therein.
O God, bless my kindred,
Bless thou my substance.
O God, bless my words,
Bless thou my converse.

Be Christ's cross on your new
dwelling,
Be Christ's cross on your new hearth,
Be Christ's cross on your new abode,
Upon your new fire blazing.
Be Christ's cross on your means
and portion,
Be Christ's cross on your kin
and people,
Be Christ's cross on you each light
and darkness,
Each day and each night of your lives.
Each day and each night of your lives.

The Journey

Alone with none but thee, my God,
I journey on my way.
What need I fear, when thou art near
O King of night and day?
More safe am I within thy hand
than if a host did round me stand.

ST COLUMBA

God be with you in every pass,
Jesus be with you on every hill,
Spirit be with you on every stream,
Headland and ridge and lawn;
Each sea and land,
each moor and meadow,
Each lying down, each rising up,
In the trough of the waves,
On the crest of the billows,
Each step of the journey you go.

Vision and Service

As the hand is made for holding
and the eye for seeing,
you have fashioned me, O Lord, for joy.
Share with me the vision
to find that joy everywhere:
in the wild violet's beauty,
in the lark's melody,
in the face of a steadfast man,
in a child's smile,
in a mother's love,
in the purity of Jesus.

Be thou my vision,
O Lord of my heart,
be all else but naught to me,
save that thou art;
be thou my best thought
in the day and the night,
both waking and sleeping,
thy presence my light.

☙

Be thou my wisdom,
be thou my true word,
be thou ever with me,
and I with thee, Lord;
be thou my great Father,
and I thy true son;
be thou in me dwelling,
and I with thee one.

8TH CENTURY IRISH
TRANSLATED BY MARY BYRNE AND ELEANOR HULL

He is a bird round which a trap is closed
A leaking ship unfit for a wild sea,
An empty vessel and a withered tree,
Who lays aside God's wishes unimposed
He is the sun's bright rays,
pure gold and fine,
a silver chalice overfilled with wine,
Holy and happy, beautiful in love –
Who does the will of God
in Heav'n above.

TRANSLATED BY MOLLY CARSON

In Difficult Times

I am weary, weak and cold,
I am weary of travelling land
and sea,
I am weary of traversing
moorland and billow,
Grant me peace in the
nearness of thy repose
this night.

At Tara today in this fateful hour
I place all heaven with its power,
And the sun with its brightness,
And the snow with its whiteness,
And fire with all the strength it hath,
And lightning with its rapid wrath,
And the winds with their swiftness
along the path,
And the sea with its deepness,
And the rocks with their steepness,
And the earth with its starkness:

All these I place
By God's almighty help and grace,
Between myself and the powers
of darkness.

ST PATRICK

As the rain hides the stars,
as the autumn mist hides the hills,
as the clouds veil the
blue of the sky,
so the dark happenings of my lot
hide the shining of your face
from me.
Yet, if I may hold your hand
in the darkness,it is enough.
Since I know that,
though I may stumble in my going,
you do not fall.

TRANSLATED BY ALISTAIR MACLEAN

Relieve thou, O God, each one
In suffering on land or sea,
In grief or wounded or
weeping,
And lead them to the house of
thy peace
This night.

Angels All Around

The maker of all things,
The Lord God worship we:
Heaven white with angels' wings,
Earth and the white-waved sea.

Thou Michael the victorious,
I make my circuit under thy shield,
Thou Michael of the white shield,
And of the brilliant blades,
Conqueror of the dragon.
Be thou at my back,
Thou ranger of the heavens,
Thou warrior of the King of all.
O Michael the victorious,
My pride and my guide,
O Michael the victorious,
The glory of mine eye.

Day and Night

With God be my walking this day,
With Christ be my walking this day,
With the Spirit my walking this day,
The Threefold all-kindly my way:
Ho, ho, ho!
The Threefold all kindly
I pray.

O God, who broughtest me
from the rest of last night
unto the joyous light of this day
be thou bringing me
from the new light of this day
unto the guiding light of eternity.
Oh! from the new light of this day
unto the guiding light of eternity.

God, a love-flame
kindle in my heart
To neighbours all,
To foe, to friend,
to kindred,
To brave, to knave,
to thrall.

A FIRE-LIGHTING PRAYER

My Chief of generous heroes,
bless my loom and
all things near to me,
Bless me in all my busy-ness,
Keep me for life
safe-dear to thee.

A PRAYER FOR WEAVING

Be blessing, O God,
my little cow,
and be blessing, O God,
my intent;
O God, my partnership
blessing thou,
and my hands that
to milking are sent.

A MILKING PRAYER

Learned in music sings the lark,
I leave my cell to listen;
His open beak spills music, hark!
Where heaven's bright
cloudlets glisten.
That God bright Heaven
may give me,
and keep me in eternal calm
And from all sin relieve me.

THE HERMIT'S PRAYER

Let the light fall warm and red
on the rock,
Let the birds sing their
evening song
and let God's people say Amen.
Amen.

❦

Let the tools be stored away,
Let the work be over and done
and let God's people say Amen.
Amen.

∂

Let the flowers close and the
stars appear,
Let hearts be glad
and minds be calm
and let God's people say Amen.
Amen.

CREATION LITURGY,
THE IONA COMMUNITY

May the Light of lights come
To my dark heart from thy place;
May the Spirit's wisdom come
To my heart's tablet from my Saviour.
Be the peace of the Spirit
mine this night,
Be the peace of the Son
mine this night,
Be the peace of the Father
mine this night,
The peace of all peace be
mine this night.
Each morning and evening of my life

Bless to me, O God,
The earth beneath my foot;
Bless to me, O God,
The path whereon I go;
Bless to me, O God,
The thing of my desire;
Thou Evermore of evermore,
Bless thou to me my rest.

In God's Presence

What can afear
With God the Father near?

Though the dawn breaks
cheerless
on this Isle today,
My spirit walks
upon a path of light.
For I know my greatness.
Thou hast built me a throne
within Thy heart.
I dwell safely within the circle
of Thy care.

A Good Death

As thou wast before
At my life's beginning,
Be thou so again
At my journey's end.

As thou wast beside
At my soul's shaping,
Father, be thou too
At my journey's close.

The shade of death lies
upon your face, beloved,
But the Jesus of grace
has his hand round about you;
in nearness to the Trinity
farewell to your pains,
Christ stands before you
and peace is in his mind.

DEATH SONG

O God, give me of your
wisdom,
O God, give me of your mercy,
O God, give me of your fullness
and of your guidance
in face of every strait.

℘

O God, give me of your holiness,
O God, give me of your
shielding,
O God, give me of your
surrounding,
and of your peace in
the knot of my death.
O give me of your surrounding
and of your peace at
the hour of my death!

Blessings

Be the eye of God
Dwelling with you,
The foot of Christ in
Guidance with you,
The shower of the Spirit
Pouring on you,
Rightly and generously.

Bless to us, O God,
The moon that is above us,
The earth that is beneath us,
The friends who are around us,
Your image deep within us.
Amen.

CREATION LITURGY,
THE IONA COMMUNITY

Acknowledgments

Thanks go to those who have given permission to include material in this book, as indicated below. Every effort has been made to trace and contact copyright owners. If there are any inadvertent omissions or errors in the acknowledgments, we apologize to those concerned and will remedy them in the next edition.

This compilation copyright © 1996 Lion Publishing

Published by
LION PUBLISHING PLC
Sandy Lane West, Oxford, England
ISBN 0 7459 3444 7
ALBATROSS BOOKS PTY LTD
PO Box 320, Sutherland, NSW 2232, Australia
ISBN 0 7324 1441 5

First edition 1996
10 9 8 7 6 5 4 3 2 1

A catalogue record for this book
is available from the British Library

Printed and bound in Singapore